to Dad with love

at Christmas time, 1985

from Larry and Diane and family

THE SAN JUAN ISLANDS

THE SAN JUAN ISLANDS

Photography by
MICHAEL BREUER

♦

Text by
ROSEMARY NEERING

SKYLINE
PRESS

Produced by Boulton Publishing Services Inc., Toronto
Designed by Fortunato Aglialoro

©1985 Oxford University Press (Canadian Branch)
SKYLINE PRESS is a registered imprint of the Oxford University Press

ISBN 0-19-540628-1
1 2 3 4 – 8 7 6 5
Printed in Hong Kong by Scanner Art Services, Inc., Toronto

All images for this book were taken
with Leica cameras and Leitz lenses,
focal lengths from 21mm to 400mm.

INTRODUCTION

The local paper is glooming about the economy but down at the waterside cafe the morning talk is of whether to spell 'liqueur' with one or two u's. Bets are laid and someone asks for a phone so they can check with the bank, 'Because they're sure to have a dictionary.'

San Juan residents are practised in not taking matters like the economy too seriously. If they'd wanted to worry about money they'd be living on the mainland, commuting on six-lane freeways, punching clocks, paying second mortgages. Instead they're catching salmon, watching the sunset, and figuring out new ways to deerproof a garden, ways that will be just as ineffective as the three dozen other ways they've tried before.

The San Juans have a way of bringing life's worries into some sort of perspective. Forty years ago Orcas Island historian Fred John Splitstone admitted, 'Almost anywhere on the northwest coast of the United States one can find better opportunities for money-making than anything the islands can offer,' but then he went on to say that 'Everyone who is physically able here works...but there is no fanaticism in the matter.'

The Lummi Indians were the first to establish this day-to-day pattern of living, getting along well enough on the bounty of the forests and the sea, and withdrawing discreetly into the woods when more bellicose bands from the north swooped down in raiding parties.

Next came the Spanish and the British, engaged in a mostly peaceful struggle for possession of the whole area. In time, faraway governments negotiated, a treaty was signed, and the Spaniards withdrew to bases further south. British traders from the Hudson's Bay Company moved in, to buy and sell, and to raise sheep, pigs and cattle.

They weren't alone for long. American prospectors, disappointed and discouraged by the 'great humbug' of the Fraser River gold rush of 1858, drifted down to the coast, crossed to the islands, set out land claims and started farming there. The treaty defining the border between British and American territory in the northwest was vague when it came to the San Juans; it said, the boundary was the middle of 'the channel' that separates the continent from Vancouver Island, but in fact at least three different channels could be so described.

Neither British nor American settlers were fanatical in their patriotic loyalties. When the British tax collector came to call, he was told he was on American land; when the American collector made his rounds, he was told he was trespassing on British territory. But pigs and their exactions were another matter. An American squatter took over some land near the Hudson's Bay Company post and planted it out with potatoes. A British pig wandered in and munched to his heart's content. 'Keep your pig out of my potatoes!' yells the American. 'Keep your potatoes out of my pig,' comes the icy rejoinder. A shot fired, a pig dead, Britain and the United States on the course to war.

Brigadier-General William S. Harney, American military commander in the northwest, longed to make his reputation on the field of battle. His adversary Sir James Douglas, recently appointed governor of Britain's colony of British Columbia, was stubborn, proud and unfailingly suspicious of Americans. Troops and warships were sent in by both sides. Armed conflict seemed unavoidable. But this was the San Juans. Fight when you could go fishing? Shoot people—when you could be shooting rabbits? Level muskets—when you could be lifting glasses? Ridiculous.

A plan was worked out for joint occupation of the islands. Harney was sent off south to the Civil War. Contingents from both the rival sides were summoned to garrison the islands and, by the time they settled in, the Pig War had taken a back seat to more important events in both countries. The soldiers made the best of a 13-year stay, competing against each other in track meets and holding parties to which all were invited. They even entertained tourists down from Victoria on a day cruise to inspect 'the field of conflict.'

The German Kaiser was asked to arbitrate and he finally awarded the islands to the United States. With no outward sign of disgruntlement, the British soldiers packed their bags and headed north.

The Pig War was the islands' moment of glory. The smugglers' area was less glorious, but it too was in the island tradition. Laws made on the mainland might dictate that certain commodities were not to be available or were to be heavily taxed, but anyone who knew the tides and passages of the heavily indented coastline of the San Juans could make his own decisions.

In the nineteenth century, the smugglers dealt in Chinese immigrants, opium and wool. The first two were transported at night in great secrecy. The trade in wool, which was much cheaper on Vancouver Island than it was in the United States, was less covert, and there would needs have been some miraculous ingredient in the pastures of the San Juans to account for the prodigious amounts of wool that were credited to the backs of the island sheep.

When Prohibition hit Washington State in 1916, four years before the rest of the country, rum runners wrote a new chapter to the smugglers' story. The tales are legion; pursuits and daring escapes, signal fires on hilltops, tricks and treachery. Even when revenue officers finally got hold of a boat that could keep up with the smugglers, and an agent as wily as the lawbreakers, more often than not the cargo would disappear into the night.

The islands attract people who don't want to live by other people's rules. One such was San Juans' first industrialist, John S. McMillin, who exploited the lime deposits on San Juan Island, building and ruling a company town and making a fortune. Even he had to be a little eccentric; he left behind in the forest a stone mausoleum, with columns, steps, stone table and stone chairs, all designed and built according to the teachings of the Masonic order.

The very definition of the San Juans obeys no rules. Some people will tell you they include only those islands in San Juan County. Others widen the definition to include the major islands of Skagit County. Some say there are 172 islands, including each one with a name. Some count everything visible at high tide, and come up with a total of 450. Some add in every rock, reef and hummock that appears at low tide—who knows how they keep track?—and put the total at 768.

Those named islands and other geographic features of the grouping bear a mixture of Indian, Spanish, British and down-home Yankee monikers that offer a quick course in the history of the area.

The Spaniards had an advantage in the naming game; they could depend upon such people as the Viceroy of Mexico, Don Juan Vicente de Guemes Pacheco Padilla Orcasitas y Aguayo, Conde de Revilla Gigedo. People like that were good for half a dozen place-names each. The British had to look further afield, though, as one historian notes, 'it were well for one coveting easy immortality to be a friend of Captain Vancouver,' the British explorer.

United States Navy men were not at all pleased with so much foreign nomenclature. In the 1830's, Lieutenant Charles Wilkes renamed almost everything he set eyes on, taking the names of friends, animals, and the appearance of geographic features as his inspiration. Fifteen years later, the British Admiralty drew up new charts and restored the old names, most of which remain today.

Some names have several stories behind them. If you're a mainlander, you'll believe that Friday Harbor, on San Juan Island, was named for Joe Friday, a Kanaka servant of the Hudson's Bay Company. Any islander, on the other hand, will tell you that Friday Harbor got its name when one ship's captain misheard another's shouted query, 'What bay is this?' Fribay, of course.

Much of the San Juans' special character comes from their physical characteristics. Like islands anywhere, they embody a sense of isolation and independence. It takes time to get to the islands, time in which to shrug off the cares that the mainland deems important.

But the San Juans are not completely isolated. The larger islands can be reached by ferries that ply the waters all year round stopping at each harbor up to ten times a day. The mainland is only an hour or two away for residents of these islands. Even aircraft now make the San Juans a routine port of call. The services give islanders a choice. They can live on a larger island, enjoying both isolation and connections, or they can live on one of the smaller islands, and rely on their own boats. They can choose to visit the mainland or they can choose to stay at home.

The islands also provide a sense of community. If you don't wave at approaching motorists on Lopez Island, you're immediately marked as a stranger. The general store, the coffee shop, the volunteer fire departments, the bulletin boards scattered in a dozen communities, are all points of connection. Need a medical clinic? Work together to get one. Are there more different denominations than churches? Share a building. Basement flooded, car stuck, someone sick? Help will probably be on hand the moment you call.

But there's more to the islands than people. Wake up on a rare frosty morning to see a heron silhouetted against the reddening sky. Glimpse Mount Baker in mist or on a clear evening. Feel your breath catch at the unmistakable sight of a whale close offshore. See the myriad forms of intertidal life. Drift on a lake, setting a fly for trout. Lean on the wind with the bent shapes of island fir on the headlands. It doesn't take long to see why people love these islands.

They love them even in summer, when crowds of boaters, bicyclists and car passengers arrive, trying for a tiny sample of island life. They love them best in spring, fall and winter, when there are no ferry lineups and no hustle and bustle.

They know the balm that the islands can offer to the spirit, and they like to recount the story of Robert Moran, Seattle shipbuilder and politician, whose doctor told him in 1904 that he had but a few months to live. Chastened, Moran sold up his holdings and sailed away to his dream islands, the San Juans. On Orcas he built a luxurious mansion in which to spend his last days. Then he built roads, a water system, an electrical system. Finally he gave away to the community most of the land he acquired over the years. Years indeed, because Robert Moran died in 1943 at the age of 86, full 40 years after his doctor's sentence of death. For islanders, there's no further explanation needed than this—that he lived on the San Juans.

ROSEMARY NEERING

1 *Sunrise and Mount Baker from American Camp, San Juan Island.* Mount Baker rises almost 11,000 feet in the North Cascades, 50 miles east of the San Juans. Set among lower mountains, its snow-covered volcanic cone is an orientation point for islanders and visitors alike.

2 *Madrona, Lopez Island.* The madrona, *arbutus menzeii*, a broad-leafed evergreen, is found only in a narrow belt that stretches from Oregon north along the coast to southern Vancouver Island. Its characteristic rough grey bark, that sheds to reveal smooth red-brown limbs, makes it unmistakeable.

3 *Mount Baker, from American Camp.* Mount Baker in the dawn, glowing faintly in the sunrise, half-hidden in the mists; Mount Baker on a frost-clear winter day, sculptured in light and shadow; Mount Baker at sunset, a landmark slowly disappearing as the last light fades. There is no sight so familiar from the San Juans as the silhouette of this volcanic peak 50 miles to the east.

4 *Lopez Island Centre Church.* This Roman Catholic church, established in 1887, is used for a variety of community functions. It is served by a travelling priest.

5 (right) *View from Mt Erie, Fidalgo Island.* Linked so definitely to the mainland by a bridge, Fidalgo seems almost not an island. Yet it too is part of the archipelago. Mt Erie, near Anacortes, is a favorite spot on the island, providing this view to the east of the farmlands of Fidalgo and, to the west, a panorama of islands stretching north and south.

6 (left) *Farmlands on San Juan Island.* The first farmers on the San Juans were the men of the Hudson's Bay Company, who established a farm on San Juan Island, where they raised sheep, cattle and pigs, and grew carrots, turnips and potatoes. Today, cattle and sheep graze most of the cleared farmlands, and crops such as hay, vegetables and fruit are grown on the fertile soil.

7 *Tulips, Lopez Island.* The gentle climate of the islands encourages gardeners. Mild winters—it's a rare winter day when the temperature stays below freezing—allow careful gardeners to cultivate plants forbidden to their neighbors on the mainland. Islanders do have other problems: salt spray, limited rainfall and ubiquitous deer. A recent San Juans almanac devotes an entire chapter to choosing plants for a deer- and drought-resistant garden.

8 *Madrona and Maple Leaves, San Juan Island.* The glow of brighter leaves breaks the overall deep green of San Juan's forest.

9 (right) *Richardson General Store, Lopez Island.* Sooner or later, everyone drops by the Richardson General Store. Although Richardson is no longer the hub of Lopez Island, the store itself carries on the tradition started 100 years ago by the first storekeeper. Galvanized washtubs hang from the ceiling; wooden clothes-pegs are for sale alongside car oil and crabtraps. A supermarket would not be ashamed of the variety of goods arranged in intricate patterns on the crowded shelves. And Richardson's ice-cream cones are a summer 'must'.

10 *Beach near Lopez Village, Lopez Island.* For over a hundred years, loggers have been at work in the forests that crowded to the water along the mainland. For far longer than that, storms have sent waves crashing onto island beaches. Many a beach is strewn with logs flung adrift in stormy weather from log booms or rolled from beach to beach by tide, wind and waves.

11 *Cattle, San Juan Valley Road, San Juan Island*. Although sheep outnumber them, cattle are a familiar sight on the grazing lands of the islands. Not just everyday breeds either: white Charolais from France and shaggy, horned Highland cattle share space with Black Angus and white-faced Herefords.

12 *Cosmos in a garden near Dewey on Fidalgo Island.*

13 (right) *House at Fisherman Bay, Lopez.* The islands were settled mostly in the late 1800s and the early years of this century, and the architecture of the remaining older houses reflects this era. Many are in Victorian style, some with 'gingerbread' work but most of them 'straight-laced' and practical, two-storey frame dwellings with verandahs and a sweetly old-fashioned air.

14 *Agate Beach, Lopez.* Lucky searchers may still find agates on some of the San Juan beaches, though most must be content with the smooth, polished stones that give the beaches color and variety.

15 (right) *Spencer Spit Park, Lopez.* Spencer Spit is a triangular wedge of sand enclosing a saltwater lagoon. Tides and waves have created the spit. In time, the lagoon may fill with sand and sediment. The spit is part of a state park that attracts bird-watchers and campers.

16 (left) *Clouds seen from American Camp, San Juan Island.* Weather watchers love the San Juans; the warm dry, land areas, the moisture absorbed into the air from the ocean, and the sea winds combine to create a changing vista of clouds, clear skies, mist, gentle rain and furious storms.

17 *Douglas fir trees, Moran State Park, Orcas Island.* They call them 'island fir', and think of them as a special hardy breed, able to resist the winds that batter them in winter and to thrive on the limited rainfall. Mainland Douglas fir are the giants of the forest, up to 200 feet tall and four feet in diameter. On the islands, they are smaller, almost uniform in height, a green mantle over hill and valley.

18 *Olga Store, Orcas Island.* You can get most anything you want at the Olga store: a beer, a conversation, a quart of milk or a moment's respite beside the oil drum stove that warms the big room. You can even—but don't tell the traditionalists!—get a container of guacamole, some Brie for your afterdinner cheese course or a gourmet TV dinner. Like other stores on the islands, Olga's, built in 1902, serves as a community centre, with notices pinned to boards and coffee always hot.

19 (right) *Roche Harbor Resort, San Juan Island.* Biographers refer to John S. McMillin as a pioneer industrialist, and that he certainly was. He created the largest lime-producing enterprise in the west, and became one of the richest men in Washington State. Less friendly folk refer to him as the epitome of 'bossism' and perhaps he was that too. He controlled his company town and the actions of everyone in it. What remains of the town at Roche Harbor, built up in the 1880s and and 1890s, is now a resort that attracts boaters from all around the Pacific Northwest.

20 *Farmland near Westsound, Orcas Island.* Farming near Westsound dates back to early squatters' claims in the 1850s, when the first white residents soon made themselves self-sufficient from products of land and sea. By 1900, the Western Trading Company was shipping livestock, grain and fruit to mainland cities. Tourism has replaced farming as a major industry, but farms still dot the valleys and gently sloping hills of Orcas Island.

21 (right) *Madrona leaves, San Juan Island.* Although the madrona is an evergreen, it seems as though some part of the tree is always falling off, much to the despair of gardeners who try to domesticate it. Leaves, bark, berries, flowers; the madrona is a confirmed litterbug.

22 (left) *Sunset over the harbor at Lopez Village.* Not surprisingly, almost every village or town in the San Juans is located at water's edge. Although routine transportation is by road, islanders are strongly linked to the sea; it's a rare island family that does not own a boat of one sort or another.

23 *Seagull, Lopez.* The islands are rich in bird life, with gulls, ducks, herons, cormorants, geese and a dozen other species ruling the sea, and bald eagles and hawks leading the list of those that prefer the land.

24 *Beach, Shoal Bight, Lopez.* This long, narrow, rocky stretch, littered with driftwood, divides Lopez Sound from Rosario Strait and connects a wooded point with the rest of the island.

25 *Fishing boats seen from South Beach, San Juan Island.* They say that in the early days of the century, the fish almost jumped into the boats, and a million or more salmon were caught in a season. Canneries, fish-packing plants and service centres were all set up on the islands to handle the catchers and the catch.

26 *Fishing Boats, Friday Harbor, San Juan Island.* Fishing is no longer the dominant industry it once was, but many gillnetters and some purse seiners still call the islands home. Most tie up at Anacortes or Friday Harbor, but it's a rare island harbor that contains no fishboats. Salmon are still the most sought-after fish, though fishermen are increasingly aware of the value of bottom fish.

27 (right) *West Beach, Whidbey Island.* Whidbey is one of those islands that might not be one of the San Juans, depending on whose definition you choose. West Beach, in Deception Pass State Park, is a microcosm of the west coast: forest, rocky beaches, sand dunes and a mecca for winter storm-watchers.

28 View from American Camp, San Juan Island. For 13 years, from 1859 to 1872, American soldiers looked out over Haro Strait from their camp atop the cliffs and wondered if they would ever have to fight their British counterparts in residence a few miles further north on the island. The joint occupation of the disputed San Juans was finally ended by arbitration and the award of the islands to the United States.

29 *Dragonfly, Moran State Park, Orcas Island.* Moran State Park is Orcas Islands' largest park, centred on Mt Constitution, at 2500 feet the best viewpoint on the San Juans. The park is an excellent site for camping, fishing, hiking and nature-watching. The land was donated by and the park named for Robert Moran, who came to Orcas to retire in 1904.

30 (left) *American Camp, San Juan Island.* These headlands stretch out well beyond American Camp, dry, grassy expanses of shifting sand dune that are unusual in the islands. The wind sweeps in here from the sea, sculpting the few trees into streamlined shapes. Cliffs drop sharply from the grassy lands to the rocks and sea below. The sandy ground provides ideal terrain for rabbits, who construct many-tunnelled warrens below ground. No one has ever counted the rabbits, but if you ask how many there are on the San Juan island, you're sure to be told, 'Too d——d many!'

31 *Beach near Cattle Point, San Juan Island.* One story suggests that this point got its name when cattle swam ashore from a boat that capsized near here. It's more likely that the name dates back to the time when the Hudson's Bay Company first introduced cattle to the island, and found this a convenient place to land them. The cattle might well have swum to land; it was easier to push the beasts overboard and watch them head promptly for shore than to try to unload them at a dock.

32 *Little Red Schoolhouse, Shaw Island.* At one time, this one-room schoolhouse, built in the 1890s, was reduced to three students. In more recent years, a dozen girls and boys in 12 grades have come each day to learn their lessons.

33 (right) *La Conner.* Not strictly on the San Juans, the town of La Conner seems to be a part of them. Its bravely painted Victorian buildings, coterie of artists and writers, and restaurants serving healthy, home-made bread and fresh seafood, are in the spirit of the San Juans, which begin just across the narrow waters of Swinomish Channel.

34 (left) *Fog and Farmland, Lopez Island.* Fog is a fact of life for the northwest coast. Sometimes it's a gentle mist, like this one that hovers above the cleared land of Lopez. At other times it can blanket shore and sea thickly enough that the deep-throated bleat of the foghorn only emphasizes the islands' isolation.

35 *Deer, False Bay, San Juan.* Many a San Juan farm is posted with 'No Hunting' signs, an indication of the deer that live happily on the islands. They thrive here, as witnessed by the high fences and nets that surround almost every garden. They're not as common, though, as they were a hundred years ago, when at least one pioneer made a good living as a deer hunter, selling meat and hides to traders.

36 *Street in Anacortes, Fidalgo Island.* Anacortes is the only city in the San Juans, and the main industrial centre. Its economic life centres on two oil refineries, a number of canneries and the construction industry. Named for Anna Curtis Bowman, wife of the founder, it is sometimes called the 'Front Door' or the 'Gateway' to the San Juans, since San Juans ferries leave from a point just beyond the city.

37 (right) *Farmland, Orcas.* The San Juans were once the major suppliers of fruit and vegetables to Bellingham and Seattle. The advent of irrigation in mainland valleys ended that era, but agricultural products are still important to the San Juans.

38 *Roche Harbor Resort, San Juan Island.*

39 (right) *La Conner.* La Conner, a small artists' and fishing village overlooking the east
side of Fidalgo Island, was founded in 1867. It
is the oldest town in Skagit County, and one of
the oldest in Washington State.

40 *Cabin, Squaw Bay Road, Shaw Island.* This cabin on Shaw, the smallest of the islands served by ferry, is no longer used as a dwelling; it has been replaced by a more modern house. The rough board, log and shake type of construction is rare among the San Juan's remaining historic buildings.

41 *Harbor, Lopez Island.* Homes and businesses cluster along the water-front. The protected harbor provides refuge for many who cruise the islands.

42 *Farm, Lopez Island.* Lopez, the flattest of the San Juan outer islands, is devoted primarily to farming. The fertile loamy soil of the island encourages the planting of crops, like the rapeseed shown here.

43 (right) *Blazing Tree Ranch, San Juan Island.* It seems strange to see a ranch on an island, but the grassy stretches of San Juan provide good grazing and hay-making territory.

44 (left) *Museum, Friday Harbor.* Friday Harbor's museum is housed in this frame house built by pioneer farmer James King in 1890, after his original log cabin burned down. It was given to the San Juan Historical Society in 1966 by then owner George Peaock and refurbished as a museum in early farmhouse style.

45 *Afterglow Vista Mausoleum, Roche Harbor, San Juan Island.* 'John Stafford McMillin, A.B.A.M., a 32 Mason, Knight Templar, Noble of Mystic Shrine, Methodist, ε.χ. Republican,' the inscription on the stone reads, encapsulating all the things that the founder of Roche Harbor found important. Designed according to the teachings of the Masonic order, the mausoleum centres on a limestone table with seats for mother, father and each child, where the family would symbolically gather in the hereafter. The broken column is intentional, representing the breaking of the string of life by death.

46 *Roche Harbor Church.* Roche Harbor Church was part of John McMillin's company town; it was built in the late 1880s along with family home, store, school, offices, warehouse and ships' repair-yard to serve a population that reached 800 at its height. Like McMillin, the church was Methodist. It was renovated and rebuilt by the Reuben Tarte family, who bought the estate in the late 1950s. Now with a new statue of Our Lady of Good Voyage sent from Italy and with new bells, it serves as a Roman Catholic chapel, with services held each Sunday in summer.

47 (right) *English Camp, San Juan Island.* In the lull that followed the Pig War, British troops built a camp beside sheltered Garrison Bay on the west coast of San Juan Island. There they remained for the more than a decade between the almost-hostilities and the formal resolution of the dispute. The original blockhouse, commisary, barracks and a maple tree that is one of the largest in the world are still on the site, which is part of the San Juan National Historical Park. In summer, park personnel in appropriate costume give guided tours and talk about the history of the area.

48 *Shoal Bight, Lopez.*

49 (right) *Richardson, Lopez Island.* Once Richardson was the busiest place in all the San Juans, as the fishing boats that thronged the strait chugged in to refuel at the best deepwater harbor on the island. Now Richardson is a little quieter, though on a summer's day when the fish are running, 150 boats can tie up to the dock where skippers can refuel and swap stories.

50 *Fishing-boat at MacKaye Harbor, Lopez.*

51 *Deadman Bay, San Juan Island.* The history of Deadman Bay is a little obscure, but stories handed down have it that the Bay was so named because the first death of a white man on the islands occurred here—a laborer murdered by a cook.

52 *Beach near Lopez Village, Lopez Island.*

53 (right) *Lopez Center Road, near Stanley, Lopez Island.*

54 (left) *San Juan Island, West Coast.* Only the hardiest of bushes survive on the rocky outcroppings that form cliffs on some parts of the San Juans. Although trees clothe most of the land that has not been cleared by human hands, some areas are barren and are home only to nesting seabirds.

55 *Red-winged blackbird and bulrushes, Hummel Lake, Lopez Island.* Much of the San Juans area receives just 20 inches of rain a year or less. Nonetheless, most islands have quiet lakes and ponds where birds and water plants abound. Motorboats are forbidden on Hummel Lake, the largest body of fresh water on Lopez Island. The lake is regularly stocked with rainbow trout.

56 (left) *False Bay, San Juan Island.* At low tide, False Bay reveals the reason for its name. Once the tide goes out, almost 200 acres of tidal flats are revealed, along with a variety of crabs, barnacles, rock oysters and other intertidal life. The bay is used as a study area by the University of Washington biology department.

57 *Fishing-nets and boats, Mackaye Harbor, Lopez Island.*

58 *Ferry, Neck Point, Wasp Passage.* From dugout canoes to steam stern-wheelers to modern ferries that bustle from island to island, the San Juans have always been dependent on boat transportation. Washington State Ferries operate between Anacortes and four of the islands: San Juan, Orcas, Lopez and Shaw, with daily runs across the Canadian border to Sidney on Vancouver Island. Ferries also connect smaller islands like Guemes with larger islands or with the mainland.

59 (right) *Farmland, San Juan Island.*

60 *Ferry landing, Shaw Island.* Going 'to town', coming home, going to see a friend across the channel, getting supplies, sending cattle—or artworks—to market...For the visitors the ferries are picturesque, an opportunity for a sea cruise but for the islanders on the main islands of the San Juans they are essential links with the outside world and with each other. On Shaw, the ferry landing is operated for most of the year by nuns who live in a convent on the island.

61 (right) *Boats in front of the Roche Harbor General Store, San Juan Island.* Boat hardware, yes, and a case can certainly be made for stocking wine. But microwave popcorn and gourmet peapods? Times have changed in the boating fraternity and the stock at the Roche Harbor General Store reflects the changes. Roche has long been a favorite stopping place for boaters; in summer, the harbor is crowded almost to the neck, with boats tied up to buoys and rafted together at the dock. Year-round, the general store serves the needs of liveaboards and cruisers alike.

62 *Library, Lopez Island.* Like many a small town library, the Lopez library is a cultural center. Staffed mainly by volunteers, it opens its doors 28 hours a week, sometimes in the morning, sometimes in the afternoon, sometimes in the evening. The latest possession is a computer, with special instruction offered by island high-school students to computer-shy older folk. The building that now houses the library was built as a schoolhouse in 1895; since then it has been restaurant, store and firehall.

63 *Reef netter, Shaw Island Museum*. Reef netting dates a long way back. Local Indians began reef netting, with dugout canoes and nets made from strips of cedar or willow bark. Modern reef netters use boats like these, with ladder-like lookouts in the bow. Two boats work together in shallow water, with a net stretched between them and weighted at the bottom, creating an artificial reef. The lookouts take up their position, and let out a shout when fish swim into the net. The net is hauled up, the catch shifted to holding nets and the procedure repeated.

64 *Congregational Church, Lopez Island.* Built in 1904, this is the village church of Lopez. Like other churches on the island, it serves more than one denomination, more than one purpose. It is perhaps better known as the Community Church.

65 (right) *Causland Park, Anacortes.* French-Canadian architect Jean Baptiste Lepage designed this memorial to the men of Fidalgo, Guemes, Decatur and Cypress islands who died in the First World War. Named for Harry Leon Causland, one of 100 immortals awarded the DSC, the park was built by volunteers. Mosaics made of local sandstone, granite and quartz decorate and form walls and a gazebo that now houses a picnic table.

66 *Cascade Falls, Moran State Park, Orcas Island.* Cascade Falls, roaring over a 100-foot-wide cliff that quickly narrows, is part of a chain of waterfalls on Cascade Creek in Moran State Park.

67 (right) *Salal and Douglas fir, Mt Erie, Fidalgo Island.* There are different opinions about salal, a low-growing evergreen bush. The florist loves it for its year-round enlivening of bouquets. The logger curses it, because its tenacious growth can make passage through a forest almost impossible. It provided a food supply for the Indians, who dried and pounded its berries into a cake. The berries are still used now, often mixed with berries of Oregon grape, to make tart jellies and jams. The deep, green, glossy leaves of salal are a familiar site in the northwest forests.

68 *Log cabin at Eastsound Museum, Orcas Island.* The cabin that now houses part of the Eastsound Museum comes from the Boede family homestead on Orcas, where land was first broken in about 1885. This cabin and several others have been moved to Eastsound. They contain a collection of Orcas Indian artefacts, antiques and memorabilia.

69 Shelter with driftwood, Spencer Spit Park, Lopez Island. This shelter is a recreation of a beach cabin that was built here more than 50 years ago. The shelter is made up partly of logs from the original cabin, partly of beach driftwood.

70 (left) *Wild rosehips, San Juan Island.* Four varieties of wild roses are among the wildflowers that grow on the San Juans. Rich in Vitamin C, the rosehips are valued by those who harvest the hedgerows, for use in rosehip syrup, jam, fruit soup, wine, tea or trail mix.

71 *Pond, San Juan Island.*

72 *Fisherman's World Market and Green Ship Inn, Anacortes, Fidalgo Island.* Fish and shipping sustained Anacortes' economy for many a decade. These businesses on Anacortes' main street testify to that part of the town's past and present.

73 (right) *Paddlewheeler* W.T. Preston, *Anacortes, Fidalgo Island.* The *W.T. Preston* plied the waters of Puget Sound for almost 40 years, keeping the waters clear for navigation. A steel-hulled snagpuller run by the US Army Corps of Engineers, she was the second to carry her name; the first, a wooden-hulled steam boat, contributed much of her equipment to her successor when she was retired in 1939. The last paddlewheeler to work the northwest sounds and straits, the *W.T. Preston* also took part in steam and sternwheel races at fairs and regattas for several decades. She was given new oil burners in 1970, then taken out of service in the 1970s. Now she sits, beached, on the waterfront in Anacortes, where she is being converted into a museum.

74 *Mountain Lake, Moran State Park, Orcas Island*. A three-and-a-half mile trail around Mountain Lake provides good views of Mount Constitution and the eagles and hawks that soar in the updrafts near the mountain.

75 (right) *Oregon grape, Moran State Park, Orcas Island*. When this plant was first discovered by botanist David Douglas nearly two hundred years ago, specimens he sent to England commanded £10 each, a mighty sum in those days. You couldn't make your fortune selling it now, but you can make yourself tart jam from its berries or plant it where its attractive holly-like leaves, clusters of yellow flowers, and dark blue berries with frosty bloom will brighten your garden year-round.

76 *Heart Lake, Fidalgo Island.*

77 (right) *Reflections in a cattle pond, Blazing Tree Ranch, San Juan Island.*

78 (left) *South Beach, American Camp.*

79 *Rosario Resort, Orcas Island.* In 1904, millionaire Robert Moran came to the San Juans to live out what the doctors told him would be the last few years of his life. Moran was still alive in 1938, when he sold Rosario, his San Juans home. In the meantime, he had built a mansion that featured teak parquet-floors, mahogany wall-panelling and staircases, a magnificent pipe organ with 1972 pipes, and stained-glass windows. Moran didn't limit himself to his home; he developed roads and gave them to the county, donated all the land for Moran State Park and developed a community water system. Rosario is now a posh resort that generates three-quarters of San Juan County's tourist revenue.

80 (left) *American Camp, San Juan Island.*

81 *Closeup, Roche Harbor, San Juan Island.*

82 *Sunset, Agate Beach, Lopez Island.*

83 (right) *Canoeing, Cascade Lake, Orcas.* Cascade Lake is the largest of the outer islands' fresh-water lakes, and the busiest. Canoeists, fishermen, hikers and campers all cluster round in summer. The lake is part of Moran State Park; trails lead from and past the lake to other sites in the park and nearby.

84 *California poppies, San Juan Island.* The California poppy is the state flower of California, but somewhere along the line its seeds escaped from cultivated gardens in the San Juans. Now its glowing orange blooms carpet the open clifftops in spring and early summer. They make their best show in sunlight; in cloud or gloom, they close their petals.

85 (right) *Deception Pass Bridge.* Fidalgo, Pass Island, Whidbey, a trio of islands just a few hundred feet apart with Deception and Canoe passes separating them. Yet for generations of would-be travellers, they might as well have been 10 miles apart. As early as 1907, local residents clamored for a bridge; the Deception Pass Bridge was completed in 1935. The cantilevered span, 182 feet high and supported in the centre by pillars on Pass Island, could not be aligned at first; workmen had to wait until cool morning air allowed the metal to contract and the sections to be joined.

86 *Sunset from American Camp, San Juan Island.* Clouds and mists gather and
change over the San Juans, making sunrise and sunset memorable times of day.

87 (right) *Limekiln Lighthouse, San Juan Lighthouse.* Limekiln warns the thousands of
boaters who travel the San Juans of the rocky cliffs that front Haro Strait. Its light
first flashed in 1919. Now fully automated, the lighthouse serves as the headquarters
of the whale research laboratory of the island's Moclips Cetological Society and a
lookout for the orcas that frequent these waters.

88 *Sunset from San Juan County Park.*